FATHER JOHN SULLIVAN SJ

BY REV FERGAL McGRATH SJ

First published in 1942 by Messenger Publications
2nd Edition 2016 by Messenger Publications

ISBN 978-1-910248-29-4

Designed by Messenger Publications Design Department
Typeset in Times New Roman
Printed by Naas Printing Ltd

MESSENGER
PUBLICATIONS
JESUITS in IRELAND

Messenger Publications,
37 Lower Leeson Street, Dublin 2
Tel: +353 1 6767491
www.messenger.ie

CONTENTS

Introduction

Donal Neary SJ

In November of 2015 Pope Francis declared Fr John Sullivan SJ Venerable. This was after many years of devotion in Gardiner Street, Dublin, Clongowes Wood College, Naas, and other parts of Ireland, particularly Newry, Co Down. The annual Mass in St Francis Xavier's Church, Gardiner Street at the anniversary of his death draws a packed church, as does the annual Mass in Clongowes in May of each year, around the date of his birth. Many cures, big and small, have been attributed to his intercession. On 27 April, 2016, Pope Francis signed the decree of his beatification, which will take place later this year in Dublin.

At a service to honour the life of Fr John Sullivan SJ, Archbishop Michael Jackson recalled in Christ Church Cathedral that Fr Sullivan spent half of his life as an Anglican and a layperson, and half as a Roman Catholic and a Jesuit priest. Dr Jackson described Venerable Sullivan as a person who 'moved from sophistication to simplicity when the majority of people seem to crave moving in the opposite direction'.

Archbishop Diarmuid Martin said of Fr John: 'the holiness of Fr Sullivan grew and developed and deepened as his life progressed … his faith was the product of two traditions and always remained so and was enriched by that fact.' Both Churches, and the Jesuits worldwide, and the many devotees of Fr John give thanks for his life, and pray that this new title will bring many others to know of him, and of Jesus Christ whom he served so well.

Any favours received through the intercession of soon-to-be Blessed Fr John Sullivan SJ should be reported to Fr Conor Harper SJ, Milltown Park, Dublin 6.

1. The Lord Chancellor's Youngest Son

Before commencing the life-story of Father John Sullivan, a brief sketch of his immediate ancestry will not be out of place. It will help to put into proper perspective his conversion to the Catholic Church, and will also answer a question which will inevitably suggest itself, namely, whence had come the Protestantism of a family of Sullivans from County Cork.

On January 19th, 1814, a strange scene was witnessed in the town of Mallow. A funeral was taking place from Mallow Castle, the seat of the Jephson Norreys family, to the Protestant graveyard, when a throng of the Catholic townsfolk appeared, headed by their parish priest Father Barry. They carried away the coffin by force and the service was finished according to the rites of the Catholic Church. The remains were those of James Sullivan, great-grandfather of Father John Sullivan. According to local tradition, he was a man who had risen from humble origins to be steward to the owners of Mallow Castle. He had been brought up a Catholic, but, on his marriage to a Protestant, Mary Fitzgerald, in 1782, he either formally became a Protestant, or at any rate allowed all his children to be brought up Protestants. His defection cost the Church dear, for in the twelve years between 1785 and 1797, he had twelve children, of whom ten survived. On his-death-bed he repented and was reconciled to the Church by Father Barry. The Protestant clergy evidently made one last effort to assert their spiritual claims over his mortal remains, with the result already seen, which was chronicled by the State Papers of the day under the heading 'Riotous conduct at James Sullivan's funeral.' (These papers were destroyed in the burning of the Four Courts, Dublin, in 1922. The facts connected with James Sullivan are preserved in a series of articles in the Journal of the Cork Historical and Archaeological Society, 1924-28, by Dr. Henry F. Twiss - a connection of the Sullivan family.)

The eighth of James Sullivan's twelve children was Edward Sullivan, who built up a prosperous wine and provision business in the main street of Mallow. His private residence, a quaint old house with projecting bow windows, is still standing, on the west of the church grounds. There, on July 10th, 1822, was born his eldest son Edward, the future Lord Chancellor of Ireland, and father of Father John Sullivan.

Edward Sullivan the younger had a remarkably brilliant career. He received his early education at the endowed school at Midleton, entered Trinity College in 1839 and was called to the Bar in 1848. Sixteen years later he was Solicitor General, then Attorney General, Master of the Rolls, and in 1883 Lord Chancellor. In 1881 he received a baronetcy. R. Barry O'Brien in his *Dublin Castle and the Irish People* says of Sir Edward Sullivan: 'No person exercised more authority in the Administration of Ireland, in his day, than this able lawyer.'

In 1850, Edward Sullivan married Elizabeth Josephine Baily, the eldest daughter of Robert Baily, a wealthy land-agent and property owner, living at Passage West, Co. Cork. The Bailys were Catholics and the future Lady Sullivan's only brother, Robert Francis, was a close friend and supporter of Father Mathew, the apostle of temperance. She had three sisters, of whom the eldest, Margaret, became the wife of John Francis Maguire, the well-known leader of the industrial revival of Cork, and founder of the *Cork Examiner*.

Edward and Bessie Sullivan had five children, of whom John was the youngest. As sometimes happened in the cases of mixed marriages before the *Ne Temere* decree it had been agreed that, in the event of there being a family the boys should be brought up Protestants and the girls Catholics. The eldest child was the only daughter, Annie, who was born in 1851. She inherited her mother's sincerely religious and charitable character and devoted her life to works in Dublin. She was deeply devoted to her youngest brother and her name recurs frequently in the history of his conversion.

Of the sons, the eldest, Edward, afterwards Sir Edward was called to the Bar, but devoted his life to literature and a remarkable hobby, the study and practice of bookbinding, on which subject he was considered one of the greatest authorities of his day. The second son, Robert, met with a tragic end at an early age. His death will be described later. The third son William, who succeeded to the baronetcy on the death of his brother Edward, in 1928, was for a time in the Army, was later called to the Bar, and acted as Resident Magistrate in various parts of the country. He was devoted to his youngest brother, John, and was present at his deathbed.

It was on May 8th, 1861, that John Sullivan was born at No. 41 Eccles Street, where his father had lived since the beginning of his legal career. In accordance with the agreement made between his parents, he was baptised on July 15th in St. George's Protestant Church, George's Place, which adjoins Eccles Street. The late Mother Dunne, of the Sacred Heart Convent, Armagh, whose family was united with that of the Sullivans by the closest bonds of friendship, used to recall how she saw Lady Sullivan weeping after the birth of John, wishing that God had sent her a girl instead, whom she would have been able to bring up in the Catholic Faith.

We have only a few fragmentary recollections of John Sullivan's childhood. The family moved again in 1863 to No. 32 Fitzwilliam Place, and Mother Dunne recalled playing with the Sullivan children in Fitzwilliam Square and how great a joy it was to her, then a little girl of about nine, when the nurse would entrust her with the perambulator of little John, who was a most winning child, always content and smiling. The late Mother Stanislaus Joseph, of the Mercy Convent, Baggot Street, whose name will occur again, remembered hearing from his sister how, as a small boy, John used to be brought down to the diningroom for dessert, and how his first remark always was, 'I want my twaret (claret)'. This reminiscence will be read with amusement by those who knew Father John in later years as a teetotaller of the most uncompromising type.

In 1873, at the age of twelve, John Sullivan entered Portora Royal School Enniskillen where his brothers had all been educated. He gave proof there of more than usual ability and in the museum at Clongowes Wood College are preserved a large number of his prizes and medals. He preserved all his life a deep affection for his old school and in particular for the headmaster, the well-known Dr. William Steele whose son, John Haughton Steele, was to enter the Catholic Church in 1910, after a lifetime of devoted work as a clergyman of the Church of Ireland. Shortly before his death, Father Sullivan wrote some reminiscences of his schooldays in which he described Dr. Steele as always heralding his approach by the shaking a large bunch of keys so that the boys had fair warning of his coming. He also recalled happy days spent on the beautiful wooded islands of Lough Erne.

In 1877 occurred the tragic death of John's second brother Robert. The Sullivans had a summer residence, Undercliffe, at Killiney on Dublin Bay. One October day Robert Sullivan accompanied by two young friends, John and Constance Exham, went out in a small sailing boat. The boat was capsized by a sudden squall. Robert Sullivan seized an oar, and swimming over to Constance Exham, gave it to her. Almost immediately he sank himself. When some fishermen from Bray arrived on the scene they found John Exham unconscious but alive. The dead body of his sister was lying across the oar, but there was no trace of Robert Sullivan and his body was never found. As will be seen later, this tragic occurrence had considerable spiritual significance in John Sullivan's later life.

2. The Best Dressed Young Man About Dublin

In 1879 John Sullivan entered Trinity College, Dublin, and took his degree in 1883, getting a Senior Moderatorship and gold medal in classics. He was favourite pupil of Professor Tyrrell, the well-known classical scholar, and it was recalled by one of his former fellow-students that Tyrrell relied on him for the elucidation of knotty points in history and archaeology, so much so that one day, when John Sullivan was unexpectedly absent, he refused to go on with the class.

The only indication which we have of John Sullivan's religious views at this time is found in an anecdote which he related to a relative a short time before his death. He told how one of the 'skips' (as the college servants, both men and women, are called), herself a Catholic, used to harangue the students on the subject of going to church on Sundays. One Sunday she attacked John Sullivan on the subject and he replied that he was tired of going to church since it meant nothing to him, but that if she would bring him to her church, he would go. Though doubtless somewhat nonplussed by this unexpected fruit of her missionary efforts, she agreed and they went together. There is no record, however, of what his impressions were, or whether he continued to go to Mass at this time. As will be seen later, he did attend Mass regularly at some period previous to his formal reception into the Catholic Church.

Sir Edward Sullivan died suddenly in 1885 and shortly after this John Sullivan left Ireland, commenced his legal studies at Lincoln's Inn and was called to the English Bar in 1888. He apparently lived on in London for some years.

Father John Sullivan, S.J.

According to Debrett for 1895, he had chambers in Lincoln's Inn and was a member of the Reform Club. There is, however, little known of his career as a barrister. He seems never to have appeared in the English courts, but he worked in chambers with Mr. R. F. McSwinny, a well-known expert in mining law, and at one time acted as Marshal to Lord Justice Mathew when on circuit. There are various recollections of his having appeared in the Irish courts in company with Judge William O'Brien at Cork, Limerick, Killarney, Carlow and Naas. It seems certain however, that he was never a member of the Irish Bar, and that on these occasions he was merely acting as registrar, a function which required no legal qualifications at all.

It was at this period of his life that he made those extensive travels which provided him with such a fund of reminiscences in later life. He did the usual continental trips, and also made walking tours in Greece, Macedonia and Asia Minor. He learned modern Greek and became intimate with the Prime Minister of Greece, M. Tricoupis, who facilitated him on his travels, even, on at least one occasion, going so far as to provide him with an escort of soldiers. About 1895 a massacre took place at Adana, in Asia Minor, and John Sullivan was one of the members of a Royal Commission set up by the British Government to enquire into it. At one period he spent several months in one of the Orthodox monasteries on Mount Athos and even thought of entering there as a monk.

When at home in Ireland, John Sullivan was a popular figure, with a touch of remoteness that marked him out from others though it did not separate him from them. Those who recollect his later poverty of dress will hardly be able to repress a smile at the description given of him by the late Father Tom Finlay, S.J., as 'the best-dressed young man about Dublin.' Judge James Murphy, a well-known figure in the legal world of the day, lived at Glencairn, a beautiful estate at the foot of Dublin mountains, well-known to later generations of Dubliners as the residence of Richard Croker, the former Tammany Boss, and even better known as the place where Orby, Croker's Derby winner, was partly trained. One of Judge Murphy's sons, the Right Hon. Mr Justice Murphy, Lord Justice of Appeal in Northern Ireland, recalled what a welcome guest John Sullivan was at Glencairn, 'I would describe him,' wrote Mr Justice Murphy, 'as a man of great taste in English literature and the classics, serious-minded, somewhat shy, and always most kindly, especially to young people.'

Another life-long friend of the Lord Chancellor was Judge William O'Brien. His niece, Miss Carrie Otis-Cox, had also many pleasant recollections of the young barrister whose shyness was the despair of the ambitious mothers of Dublin society, who in vain angled for this desirable son-in-law. She recalled also his fervour after his reception into the Church, and how, when her uncle died in 1899, John served the Mass which was celebrated in the house in Merrion Square and edified all by his saintly look and demeanour. Something will be said later of John Sullivan's love of his mother, and Miss Otis-Cox remembered hearing from her uncle how, when Lady Sullivan died, John put armfuls of white lilies into her grave.

Another interesting reminiscence was given by Mrs Esther O'Kiely, wife of Professor O'Kiely of University College, Dublin. She recalled an incident, seemingly trivial, but which evidently encouraged John Sullivan on his journey towards the Catholic Church. It occurred in 1894, when he was stopping at Glencar Hotel, which was the home of Mrs O'Kiely. She was then a little girl and had a governess to teach her. One day Mr Sullivan passed by the open window of the schoolroom and stopping, enquired what lessons were going on. On being told that it was catechism, he asked if he might listen. Sitting on the window-sill, he waited until the end of the lesson and then asked if he might take away the Butler's Catechism which was being used.

Next day he returned to the schoolroom and listened again to the instruction, asking questions, rather to the alarm of the little girl. This went on all during his stay and was repeated when he returned the following summer. Mrs O'Kiely recalled that by this time her shyness had worn off and the big man was a welcome guest to the school-room. At that time, though not yet a Catholic, he used to go to Mass regularly. He did not return again to Glencar, but for many years afterwards he would send at Christmas a present of some religious book to his little fellow student of Christian doctrine.

Our knowledge of John Sullivan's spiritual life before his entrance into the Church is, unfortunately, meagre. However, it is interesting to note that he had already developed a virtue which was afterwards to be one of his most striking ones, love of the poor. His father's and his own great friend, Judge Murphy, was a very charitably-minded man. From him he learned the practice, when asked by a poor man for alms, of not merely assisting him financially, but of stopping on the road to talk to him, hearing his troubles and giving him a word of sympathy. When the news of his reception into the Church reached Dublin, a Presbyterian friend accosted Judge Murphy, who was a staunch Protestant. 'Did you hear,' he asked, 'that your friend John Sullivan has become a Catholic?'

'Don't worry,' replied the Judge good-humouredly, 'John Sullivan would go to heaven even if he became a Presbyterian.'

3. A Mother's Prayers

It was on December 21st, 1896, that John Sullivan was received into the Catholic Church by Father Michael Gavin, S.J., at Farm Street, the well-known residence of the Jesuits in London.

A few incidents have already been mentioned which may have contributed in some slight degree to his conversion, but nothing certain is known concerning the motives that led him to take the final step. It is quite likely that he spoke of them to some of his brothers in religion, but there was no common knowledge of them, not a very surprising fact to those who knew Father John's intense humility and dislike for talking about himself.

It is quite certain, however, that the prayers and example of his mother played a powerful part in his conversion. He often acknowledged this in letters and in conversation. The following passage occurs in a letter written by him in 1913 to the mother of a boy of seventeen, Jack O'Riordan, who had died at Clongowes a few weeks previously:

'I owe everything in the world to my mother's prayers and so know the power of a mother's prayer, especially in the hour of sorrow. I can form some idea of your anguish from what I saw of my own dear mother when her best-loved son and the one whom she almost idolized was taken from her at the age of twenty-four without a moment's warning. She never saw his face again and never even had the satisfaction of weeping at his grave for his remains were never found. I cannot tell you what agony she endured during the days after his loss, hoping against hope that his remains might be recovered. I believe that only for her passionate love of Our Lord and for her boundless faith, she would have lost her reason. To her prayers at that time and to her resignation to God's will I believe I owe everything, and God alone knows how much that means.'

All his life Father Sullivan had a remarkable devotion to St. Augustine and St. Monica. No doubt this was largely due to the similarity which he perceived between his own conversion and that of the great Doctor of the Church who confessed that he owed all to 'the faithful and daily tears' of his mother. He could quote long passages from the saint's works and hardly ever preached without making some reference to him.

John Sullivan's life as a Catholic was marked by unusual fervour even while he remained in the world. His mother had a much trusted companion, Miss O'Neill, who recalled how, on returning home after his reception into the Church, he went straight up to his room and stripped it of everything that might appear luxurious, contenting himself with the plainest furniture and a carpetless floor. As has been already mentioned, he had been fastidious to a degree in his dress. Now his silk underwear was replaced by ordinary linen, and his supply of ties, in the choice of which he had been inordinately particular, was reduced from a couple of dozen to a few of the plainest pattern.

From the beginning of his life as a Catholic, John Sullivan seems to have felt himself to be called to the priesthood. There is no record of how the interior call came to him but he spoke openly of his leanings to his friends. Amongst these friends were some members of the Jesuit Order who were constant visitors at his father's house, notably Father James Cullen, founder of The *Sacred Heart Messenger* and the Pioneer Total Abstinence

Association. According to Father Cullen, John Sullivan's first leanings were towards the Franciscan Order, no doubt owing to his love of poverty. However, the counsels of his Jesuit friends inclined him to join their ranks, and his inclination received further encouragement through his association with two well-known charitable institutions in Dublin.

Within a short while from his entrance into the Catholic Church, the young barrister became a constant visitor to the Hospice for the Dying at Harold's Cross, which is under the care of the Irish Sisters of Charity. An old sister, Sister Mary Linus, remembered him as 'a lovely young gentleman,' and in this case the phrase was no mere kindly cliché. He had a remarkable gift for putting the patients into good humour and showed special sympathy towards the old, bringing them tins of snuff or packages of tea, and reading for them from religious books.

Sister Mary Francesca, a sister of the poet-patriot, Tomas MacDonagh, was then a very young nun teaching in the schools attached to the hospital. Mr Sullivan used to visit the schools also, especially the night school. Characteristically, he was most interested in the poorest of the children, and on occasions came to the rescue by bailing them out in court when, in their professional capacity as flowergirls or fish-vendors they had got into grips with the law. In the course of his visits, John Sullivan formed many friendships with the nuns, several of whom advised him to enter the Society of Jesus, for which his character and talents seemed suited.

The other charitable work in which John Sullivan became interested at this time was the Night Refuge conducted by the Sisters of Mercy, in Brickfield Lane, to which are attached elementary schools. The story of his introduction to these good nuns is an amusing as well as an edifying one. Some time during the year 1898, the Mother Superior, Sister Mary Ursula Mooney, happened to be in difficulties over a sum of forty pounds which was due for bread for the Refuge. A Carmelite Father from Clarendon Street, hearing of her embarrassment, remarked that he knew someone who would come to her assistance. A few days later, a slight, handsome young man rang at the door, handed in an envelope containing twenty-five pounds in banknotes and disappeared without a word. This happened again, and the Secretary to the Mother Superior, filled with a holy curiosity as to the identity of the donor, laid an ambush for him. She arranged that, if he came again, the portress was to inveigle him into the hall and close the door. All went according to plan. The Sister Secretary was summoned and Mr John Sullivan was revealed as the benefactor.

From that on, he frequently assisted the convent. The Sister Secretary, afterwards Mother Stanislaus Joseph, Mother Superior of the Mercy Convent, Lower Baggot Street, had been reared near the Jesuit novitiate at Tullabeg and often spoke to Mr Sullivan about it. He took a special interest in the nuns' school, where there were about 1,500 pupils, mostly children of workmen in Guinness's brewery. There was in the Infant School a little girl named Annie between three and four years old. Sister Stanislaus Joseph taught her to say 'God bless Mr Sullivan and make him a holy Jesuit'. Whenever he visited the school, this mite used to seize on any book that came handy, run up to him and pretend to read out from its pages this pious and unambiguous wish. He was amused and delighted, and used to say, 'Say it again, Annie, say it again.'

On another occasion the good Sister thought things were moving rather slowly, and sent Mr Sullivan a bogus telegram to, Fitzwilliam Place. It ran as follows:

A block of marble wanted in Tullabeg to be carved into a statue to fill a niche in heaven. Phidias and Praxiteles await reply.

Ignatius Loyola, S.J.

Phidias and Praxiteles were the Master of Novices and his Socius.

John Sullivan replied with another telegram:

To St. Joseph, c/o Sr. Stanislaus Joseph.

Material not up to sample. Phidias and Praxiteles on strike; several chisels broken. General confusion in workshop. Kindly send or call at once for parcel.

Ignatius Loyola, S.J.

For two more years the consciousness of his vocation kept growing. Finally one day in autumn 1900, Miss Sullivan came in jubilation to the convent at Brickfield Lane to announce the news that John had shaved off his moustache and was going to the Jesuit novitiate at Tullabeg. He came later himself to say goodbye and seemed depressed. It was, of course, at nearly forty years of age, and after only four years in the Church, a momentous step. Some time later, his brother, Sir Edward, went down to see him and found Lord Justice Mathew's late Marshal scuffling the front gravel.

4. The Middle-Aged Novice

John Sullivan commenced his novitiate on September 7th, 1900, in the house which is officially known as St. Stanislaus' College, Tullamore, but more popularly known as Tullabeg, from the name of a small hill in the vicinity. It stands some seven miles from the town of Tullamore and was famous as a college for boys in the early years of the last century.

It was providential that John Sullivan should have as his Master of Novices a man of outstanding holiness, the late Father Michael Browne, S.J. A deep mutual esteem sprang up between them. It was obvious that John Sullivan modelled himself considerably, even in his outward demeanour, on Father Browne, and in his turn Father Browne valued highly this middle-aged novice who led the way in observing all the small customs intended to develop self-control and detachment which must have been more than ordinarily difficult to one who had developed fixed habits of life.

Those who were his fellow-novices were unanimous in their testimony to his fervour and goodness of heart. A few extracts may be quoted from the recollections of one of them.

'His simplicity and earnestness about every detail were amazing. There was never the least sign of superiority, never the least suggestion that he knew far more than the rest of us put together. In recreation he would listen with interest to anything we had to say, and if conversation lagged he always came to our assistance with stories of his travels. He knew St. Augustine by the yard and the Fioretti of St. Francis inside out.

'If after some duty or work any of us asked Brother Sullivan how he had got on, he would shake his head and shrug his shoulders and say, "I made an awful fool of myself, an awful fool of myself." This phrase became a regular catchword among us for some time. I remember during one winter the joints of his fingers got very badly cracked and bled profusely. He always refused to put anything on them to cure them. Some novices said he used to rub sand into them to make them worse.'

On 8th September, 1902, John Sullivan took his first vows as a Jesuit in the domestic chapel at Tullabeg. On these occasions every Jesuit scholastic is given a crucifix known as the vow crucifix. John Sullivan requested that he might be allowed to take as his vow crucifix one which he had brought with him to the novitiate and which had belonged to his mother. This crucifix, a brass one about nine inches high, he carried with him constantly all his life and he held it in his hands at the moment of his death.

On the completion of his novitiate, John Sullivan was sent for two years of philosophical studies to St. Mary's Hall, Stonyhurst, which was at that time the philosophical seminary for the scholastics of the English province of the Jesuit Order. He then studied theology at Milltown Park, Dublin, in preparation for his ordination. These five years were necessarily somewhat uneventful, yet even at that early stage Mr John Sullivan began to stand out as a man of unusual virtue. There are many testimonies as to his extraordinary faithfulness to Rule and his love of prayer. Remarkable, too, was that unselfish kindness that characterized him all through life. One student returned after a day's fishing, weary and wet to the skin, to find a blazing fire greeting him in his room. Another, returning home from hospital in a run-down and depressed state, found his room swept, his bed made and his fire lighted whilst he was absent at Mass. Such incidents were of common occurrence and the self-effacing Samaritan was always found to be Mr John Sullivan.

Father Sullivan was ordained by Archbishop Walsh, in the chapel at Milltown Park, on Sunday, July 28th, 1907. His first Mass was said at the convent of the Irish Sisters of Charity, Mount St. Anne's, Milltown, and his second at the Carmelite monastery, Firhouse, Tallaght. A former fellow-novice accompanied him to Firhouse and assisted at his Mass. There was benediction afterwards and Father John had difficulty in putting the Blessed Sacrament into the monstrance, a not infrequent accident with monstrances of peculiar make. There was an awkward delay of about five minutes. When he came into the sacristy after benediction his friend said encouragingly that he had got on very well. 'I made an awful fool of myself,' said Father John. It was the old catch-word of the noviceship and uttered with all the old sincerity.

Immediately after his ordination Father Sullivan was appointed to the teaching staff at Clongowes Wood College, where he was to spend most of the rest of his life. He went there that same autumn.

Before he left Milltown Park an incident occurred which foreshadowed many such in his life. During his three years of theology he had been a constant visitor to the Royal Hospital of Incurables at Donnybrook. One of the female patients there had long been suffering from lupus in the head. The disease had begun to affect her mind and preparations were being made to remove her to a mental home. Father Sullivan came on one of his visits. It was probably just after his ordination, as it is recalled that he gave many patients his blessing. He was asked to visit the sufferer from lupus and remained a long time praying over her. The next day her mind was completely restored and remained so until her death.

5. 'We Call Him The Saint, Mum'

The years 1907 to 1919 were spent by Father Sullivan at Clongowes, with an interval of one year when he returned to Tullabeg for his tertianship, a year of spiritual renovation made by all Jesuit priests shortly after ordination. His work at Clongowes fell into three categories. He taught, mainly Classics and Religious Knowledge, he was Spiritual Father to the boys, and he worked in the small public church attached to the college. Something will be said later about all of these activities.

It is a common experience that good scholars are often not good teachers and this was, to a considerable extent, true of Father Sullivan. He found it hard to understand the difficulty that his beloved Latin authors presented to mediocre boys and was inclined to let his enthusiasm outrun the ability of his class to follow. But he was most devoted and hard-working and had the reputation of being able to pull even the most backward candidate through his matriculation. The boys attributed his success more to his prayers than to his powers as a teacher, perhaps with justice.

He was fortunately blessed with a quick sense of humour, which saved him from taking too seriously the lack of response with which his enthusiasm for classical learning occasionally met. On one occasion he gave a dramatic description of the death of Shelley and wound up with the finding of a volume of Sophocles in the drowned poet's pocket. One of the class, later a distinguished Dublin surgeon, was heard to growl, 'Served him right!' alluding, it would appear, less to Shelley's other shortcomings than to the crowning folly of carrying Greek plays about in his pocket. A quick smile came to Father John's face.

In his capacity as Spiritual Father, the word veneration is hardly too strong to use of the sentiments entertained towards him by every generation of Clongownians since 1909. It is, perhaps, the most accurate word, too, for it indicates the natural shortcomings which he had as a boys' man, and over which his holiness triumphed. Veneration does not involve intimacy, rather it excludes it. Father John probably never understood boys perfectly. He took the keenest interest in them, an interest which could only have been prompted by a sincere affection. He was always at their disposal. He corresponded with, and helped many of them in later life. Yet one felt, when hearing him talking of them, that his vision of them, though clear, was from without. He was somewhat severe in his judgment of them, characterizing as 'audacious' - a favourite adjective of his what others would accept as the normal failings of healthy boyhood. But if his judgment sounded at times severe, he was never severe in heart or action. On the contrary, boys flocked to him for consolation in their troubles. His confessional was always crowded and usually by the least law-abiding citizens of the little world of school.

It was a striking example of the conquering power of true holiness. There is in the hearts of Irish boys a peculiarly responsive chord that throbs in answer to the call of the supernatural, and there was such a call in the very sight of that familiar figure, the head ever bent in prayer as he walked, the worn, emaciated face and hands, the threadbare garments, the low hurried voice that took on a peculiar ring when it spoke of God. The boys of every generation took it for granted, in their speech and letters, that he was a saint. During his last illness, one of them wrote home to his mother: 'Father Sullivan (we call him the Saint, Mum) is dying. By the time this letter arrives, he will probably be in heaven'. And the day after his death another remarked to a master, 'Sir, isn't it a great thing to be able to say that you were taught by a saint? And the funny thing is that we knew it even when we pulled his leg a bit'.

Many of his former pupils have put on record their impressions of him at different periods of his career as a schoolmaster. A few excerpts may be quoted from the reminiscences of Captain Sidney B. Minch, who was captain of Clongowes in 1911-12.

'The many visits which I paid to his room involved a certain amount of suffering for me. I lost my play-hour and in winter I knew that I had to face a cold and chilly room. Once I arrived a little before him, and did my best with the fire, which seemed to consist of a little smoke in the centre of a grate half-filled with slack. It was hopeless, and always the same. I found out also how little covering he had on his bed. It was run on the same lines as the grate half-filled with slack.

'I found Father John at best on his walks. With his hat crushed any old way under his arm, he started in a half-run, head well forward, praising everything that nature had to show. How he talked! He found out what you were interested in and then brought God or some saint right into the middle of it so naturally that even our young minds became aware of his constant preoccupation with the things of God. Every now and again he would slip aside to visit some poor folk living in a humble cottage. We would see him kneeling at the feet of the invalid. As a matter of fact, he always knelt with us to hear our confessions also.

'I knew him even better when I left Clongowes, during the Great War, and afterwards when I fetched him from Rathfarnham to help my father during his last moments on earth. I remember him well, kneeling at the bedside, his socks, which were badly shrunk, just slightly above his boots - you could actually see his shins. Before he left I realized for the first time how happy an event death could be. In the same old clothes which he always wore, he assisted at my marriage and disappeared immediately it was over.

'His memory is always vividly before me. I had a tremendous affection for him, and I know how easy it would be to exaggerate in writing about him, and how much he would hate it. I have, therefore, kept accurately to what I remember of him. There is one thought which today I still carry with me and which he alone gave me. It is this, "You'll never have to fight alone in this world, although we leave our Divine Saviour to fight alone constantly".'

The long hours which Father Sullivan spent in prayer and his constant visits to the sick and suffering did not prevent him from playing his part fully in the life of the community. He was always at the disposal of the Prefect of Studies for extra work and would cheerfully step into a gap and take any class, no mean test of virtue even for one who is not a septuagenarian. On a wet half-holiday, rather than leave the boys on their prefect's hands, he would volunteer to take a couple of classes for a walk.

His unfailing good humour made him a most pleasant companion in spite of his retiring nature. He had a highly developed sense of humour and a fund of witty anecdotes connected with the Bench and the Bar. A favourite story of his was that of a charming young lady who found herself placed beside a very serious judge at a banquet.

She tried to engage him in conversation, but could find no congenial topic. At length she played her trump-card - the great man must be musical, she thought. 'Has your Lordship heard Madam Cavallcani sing *The Voice of the Zephyr*?' 'No, thank God,' was the gruff response.

Nor was Father John's humour confined to anecdotes. On one occasion a fellow-Jesuit referred to a certain lady as Miss So-and-so. Father John, running his hand through his hair and giving his friend one of his half-shy, half-humourous looks, remarked, 'Would you call her "Miss"? She was married three times'.

It was remarkable that although Father Sullivan was so seriously-minded, and although his conversation often ran on not over-cheerful topics such as death-bed scenes and painful illnesses, he always gave the impression of being perfectly cheerful and even light-hearted. He had a quaint way of saying, 'Cheer up, cheer up, cheer up,' and his eyes would light up in a kindly fashion contrasting markedly with his rugged ascetical face. He did indeed himself give the impression of possessing that happy equanimity which comes from undiluted goodness and indifference to the things of the world.

6. The Friend of the Afflicted

If the holiness of Father Sullivan was so apparent to the careless eyes of schoolboys, it was no wonder that it attracted to him countless men and women who were learning the bitter lessons of the larger school of life. It is only possible here to dwell briefly upon the wonderful apostolate which he exercised among the sick and suffering in the countryside around Clongowes, and amongst an ever-widening circle of others whom he visited in hospitals and consoled by letter, or who came to him from almost every county in Ireland to ask the intercession of his prayers in their illnesses and misfortunes. One must speak with all the reserve required by the Church of the numerous cures and other favours attributed to his prayers. It is undoubted that extraordinary faith in the powers of his intercession was manifested not only amongst the people in the vicinity of Clongowes, but throughout Ireland.

The instances which follow are but a few selected from the many recorded. Space also demands that they should be outlined briefly, details being omitted which would render them more striking.

Though there is good reason to believe that Father Sullivan was sought after by invalids quite early in his life as a priest, the large majority of the cures recorded occurred from 1920 on. However, in 1911, only four years after his ordination, the following remarkable incident took place.

A boy named Jeremiah Hooks, living in Naas, and aged twelve at the time, was attacked by St. Vitus' dance. The disease was so bad that he was unable to use a knife or fork or even drink out of a glass or cup, as everything was jerked out of his hand. He was brought to Father Sullivan, who blessed him and assured his father he would never have the trouble again. On returning home, he sat down to a meal and his mother could not restrain her tears when she saw him use a knife and fork without difficulty. The trouble never returned and he grew up strong and healthy.

In 1918 the late Mr W. T. M. Browne, a well-known veterinary surgeon living in Naas, County Kildare, was at death's door with double pneumonia and a dangerous complication. Father Sullivan came and prayed over the unconscious invalid who very soon regained consciousness and made a complete recovery, living on until 1941. His work done, Father Sullivan slipped away before anyone could observe him, and walked back eight miles to Clongowes, though it was raining heavily.

In the spring of 1919, a woman living in Co. Carlow had been suffering from a swelling on the breast. She was threatened with an operation, which she dreaded lest her children, some of whom were very young, should be left motherless. She wrote to her son, who was employed at Clongowes, and the letter asked Father Sullivan to say Mass for her. Father Sullivan promised to say Mass the next day, adding, 'and she will be all right in a few days'. The Mass was said on a Tuesday and on the Wednesday morning the patient, on waking, found that the swelling had completely disappeared. This woman lived until 1940 and never again felt the slightest return of the trouble.

After Father Sullivan's death, Mrs Cruise, now living at Tullamore, gave an account of the cure of her mother, Mrs Williams, who in 1922 was suffering from cataract of both eyes. A specialist had pronounced that nothing could be done. Father Sullivan came to see her and touched her eyes with a relic of Mother Aikenhead, foundress of the Irish Sisters of Charity. She rapidly recovered her sight and could read and sew without difficulty up to her death eleven years later. On examination, her eyes were found to be completely free from cataract.

In 1932, Mrs Dyer of Sutton, County Dublin, then Miss Nellie Coyne, met with an accident, as a result of which a large splinter entered her hand. The hand became very painful, but the doctors were unable to locate the splinter, even with the help of an x-ray examination. Father Sullivan was asked to bless her hand and two days later the splinter, almost as large as a match, was found protruding from the wound.

A serious fire occurred in Mary Street, Dublin, in 1925, and one of its victims was Mrs Brennan of Dublin, who, in trying to escape, fractured her leg badly. After five months in hospital, four plaster casts had failed to unite the fracture and there was danger that amputation might be necessary. Father Sullivan came to the hospital and blessed the leg, telling Mrs Brennan to pray to St. Anne. When the fifth cast was removed the bone had united perfectly and, what the doctors did not expect, there was no trace of lameness afterwards.

A remarkable cure, marked by that peculiar confidence that Father Sullivan sometimes displayed, was that of Mrs Domigan, then living at Brannoxtown, County Kildare. In 1928, being then a very young married woman, she fell into bad health and was certified by the local doctor as suffering from tuberculosis and heart trouble. She was about to go to Peamount Sanatorium, but first went to visit Father Sullivan at Clongowes, as she felt very much leaving her young children. He blessed her, and said,

'The home won't be broken up. You will be united soon again'. When she arrived at Peamount no trace of tuberculosis could be found. She returned home and has been in perfect health ever since.

In the same year occurred the cure of Michael Collins, a nephew of Michael Collins, and then a little child of three years old. His parents, Mr and Mrs Seán Collins, were then living at Celbridge, County Kildare. On October 8th the child was attacked by what appeared to be infantile paralysis, his leg being completely bent up and causing him intense pain. The local doctor and a Dublin specialist took a serious view of his case. Some workmen advised Mr and Mrs Collins to seek the help of Father Sullivan. Mrs Collins drove to Clongowes and Father Sullivan promised to say Mass for the child. Next day he was brought to the Mater Hospital and his condition remained unchanged for some days. On Tuesday, October 16th, Mrs Collins, to her surprise, received a postcard from Father Sullivan saying that he had seen Michael and that he was going home well. She hurried to Dublin and on entering the hospital was told by the nun in charge that the child was completely cured. Father Sullivan had arrived the preceding evening on his bicycle from Clongowes (he was then sixty-six, be it noted). He prayed for a long time over the child and touched his leg. When he had gone, the nun thought the child looked better, took him out of bed and put him into a warm bath. Immediately he kicked out quite normally with the leg which had hitherto been useless. The trouble never recurred and the boy grew up strong and well.

Perhaps the most remarkable of all the cures attributed to Father Sullivan occurred in December, 1932, only two months before his death. It was that of Mrs X, a young married woman, who was suffering from pernicious vomiting to a peculiarly dangerous degree. The doctor who attended her, a well-known Dublin specialist, stated that for weeks it had been impossible to feed her naturally. She had become practically a living skeleton and was in a dying condition. She was anointed on December 17th. Her sister brought Father Sullivan to see her on December 22nd. She was only half-conscious and disinclined for religious consolation. Father Sullivan sprinkled her with holy water and said a few prayers. Next day she seemed slightly better. On Christmas Eve she took toast and tea, and for the first time for weeks was able to retain the food. On Christmas Day, to the amazement of the doctor, she was able to partake of the usual Christmas dinner of turkey and ham, and from that on never looked back until she had completely recovered.

In addition to bodily cures, many cases of spiritual healing were attributed to Father Sullivan. A certain Miss X, who had known him well, went to America about 1915. When she arrived there, she found to her sorrow that her brother and sister-in-law, with their six children, had not been to the sacraments for some years. She wrote home to Father Sullivan. He said Mass for the family and on either that day or the next day they travelled a considerable distance up to San Francisco, received the sacraments and remained faithful to their religion afterwards.

A striking conversion was that of a man who was dying in a town near Clongowes. He had refused to see a priest, though urged to do so by the doctor who was attending him, the late Dr. Charles O'Connor of Celbridge. Dr. O'Connor, who was a great personal friend of Father Sullivan, called over to Clongowes and asked him to see the sick man. Father Sullivan was unable to go, but promised to say Mass for him at nine o'clock the next morning. At nine-thirty that morning, the man of his own accord asked for a priest and was prepared for death, which took place that day.

There were other instances in which Father Sullivan seemed to secure for sick persons the gift of freedom from physical pain or mental suffering, even though a cure did not follow. About 1913 Father Sullivan was asked by Mr Peter Coonan, a near neighbour of Clongowes, to visit his uncle, Thomas Coonan, who was dying of a bleeding cancer of the throat at his home in Kilclough, near Straffan, Co. Kildare. Mr Peter Coonan drove Father Sullivan over in his gig, and when they got near the house they could hear the sick man moaning and crying out in a most distressing way. Father Sullivan prayed over him for a considerable time. He then rose to go and said, 'Good-bye, Tom, and I promise you one thing, that you won't suffer any more'. Thomas Coonan died about a fortnight later and never suffered any pain after Father Sullivan's visit. The extraordinary change in his condition was a subject of comment by many neighbours, still living, who visited him.

Father Sullivan's self-sacrifice in these works of mercy was boundless. In 1929 John Nevin, who lived at Betaghs-town, near Clongowes, was dying of cancer of the face. The malady had worked terrible ravages, almost entirely destroying one side of the face. The doctor who attended the case recalled it as one of the worst he had known and found it difficult himself to approach the patient. During the last five weeks of this man's life, Father Sullivan used to visit him every day, and during the last fortnight twice a day. He used to kneel beside his bed for a considerable time, and the doctor recalled his amazement at seeing

Father Sullivan leaning right over the sufferer, with his face almost touching his. A relative added the striking detail that Father Sullivan seemed to have no fear of the cancer and would put his arms round the poor man in his bed.

On another occasion he was summoned to attend a sick person at Ballymore-Eustace, fourteen miles from Clongowes. The family were too poor to provide a car and apparently Father Sullivan had no bicycle at his disposal on that occasion. He immediately set out and walked the whole fourteen miles, returning presumably in the same manner.

This apostolate of the poor, the suffering and the afflicted never flagged during thirty years. Father Sullivan was a great cyclist and a great walker, and his figure was a familiar one on the roads around Clongowes or in the Dublin streets during his time at Rathfarnham, laboriously pedalling his dilapidated bicycle or hurrying along with his peculiar half-running gait. But, though it may seem a bold statement, it can be said confidently that he was never on any occasion seen going anywhere except to visit some sufferer or to perform some spiritual work. This feature of his life was aptly summed up on the day of his funeral by one of the farm hands in Clongowes who said, 'He seemed to take everyone's sorrow and suffering on himself'.

The secret of Father Sullivan's power to succour the afflicted was not hard to detect. A poor woman once spoke to a Sister of Charity of her intention of going to visit him in the hope of getting cured of cancer of the face. The nun asked what particular virtue this priest had over others. 'He is quite an exception,' said the woman earnestly. 'He is very hard on himself. You have to be hard on yourself to work miracles. And he does it.'

Father John Sullivan, S.J.

That his life was one of constant self-denial can be testified to by his religious brothers and the workmen and servants in Clongowes who were constant witnesses of his daily life. Every day he spent many hours before the Blessed Sacrament, and a great part of the night went to prayer also. One workman recalled having to work through the night on a damaged pipe and finding Father Sullivan in the chapel at 2.00 a.m. The same witness saw him on another occasion kneeling for about two hours in the college cemetery though a bitter east wind was blowing. On Holy Thursday about 1925, Father John approached a young scholastic and offered to take his hour of watching at the Altar of Repose. Later the scholastic found that Father John had relieved all the other scholastics of their obligation, thus taking on himself five or six hours of continuous prayer during the night. The servant who looked after his room for about a year noticed that the bed was used only every second night. There are several stories of persons having accidentally discovered Father John at his prayers long after midnight when he was giving retreats.

His room, which he always swept himself, was devoid of comfort. The servants recalled his old and broken water-jug and what they called his apology for a fire. Those in charge of his laundry related that during later years he wore only a thin flannelette shirt, even in the coldest weather. He had no overcoat, only a waterproof, old and discoloured, and he was never known to use an umbrella or to wear gloves. His boots were old and patched, and he had only one pair. Once he horrified a friend by appearing at a funeral in a pair of old slippers. He apologised and explained that his boots were being repaired. During a retreat given in the convent at Clane, near Clongowes, he used to change into slippers on his arrival. The lay-sister who was looking after him examined his boots and found what she described as 'a handful of small pebbles' in each of them. His clothes, though neat and clean, were patched beyond description, often by himself. When he travelled, the only luggage he brought consisted of his toilet articles which he stowed away in the pockets of his venerable waterproof.

In food he was abstemious to a degree. His mortification in this matter was at its height when he was Rector of Rathfarnham Castle. The students there observed that his breakfast consisted of a large plate of porridge with milk and some dry bread, his dinner of potatoes and bread, and he took no other meal. Numerous witnesses in convents agreed that his diet, when giving retreats, consisted of a cup of tea in the mornings, a small rice pudding for dinner, and a cup of tea with dry bread in the evening. After his return to Clongowes in 1924 he was ordered to eat more, and added boiled eggs and bread and butter to his breakfast. But he never ate meat and on greater feasts frequently dined on dry bread only.

7. The Preacher by Practice

Father Sullivan gave many retreats in convents and other religious houses throughout Ireland. The impression made by him everywhere was both deep and lasting. It was, however, the unanimous testimony of all who heard him that what made his retreats so memorable was not the instructions which he gave, but the example of the man himself. Briefly, he preached no virtue which he did not practice himself in a high degree. The following typical extract from letters received after his death could be multiplied indefinitely.

'We had the privilege of having Father Sullivan here (the Sacred Heart Convent, Armagh) several times. Invariably a postcard would arrive on the day before stating that he needed no car to meet him at the station and would only require a cup of weak tea. His first question on arriving was "Have you any sick in the house? and once when the answer was, Thank God, the infirmaries are empty," he remonstrated almost indignantly, "Don't say 'thank God' - the sick are a blessing in the house". He was indeed devoted to them and during his stay in the convent he visited them every day.

'He gave us the impression of being a very holy man, closely united with God. It was enough to see him come in to give an instruction, his crucifix in his hand, to feel recollected and filled with devotion. He must have had the gift of tears, for he gave us a beautiful instruction on Holy Tears and seemed to speak from experience. He several times broke down in the middle of an instruction when speaking of the love of God, the love of our Lord for sinners.'

Father John Sullivan, S.J.

From the Ursuline Convent, Waterford, where for many years he was extraordinary confessor, there came the following impressions:

'Father Sullivan's love for the Blessed Sacrament, to which he seemed to be drawn as steel to the magnet, was so great that it was with difficulty he could be induced to leave his thanksgiving after Mass. When the Sister, after some delay went to call him for his breakfast, he was usually found making the Way of the Cross. Then when she thought he was following her to the parlour for breakfast, he would be seen hastening to visit a Calvary which stands in the grounds.

'An unwonted atmosphere of prayer, calm and recollection seemed to pervade the house during Father Sullivan's visit as extraordinary confessor. It was the unconscious reflex of his own deep, simple spirituality, for he was ever an adept at self-effacement. He seemed to seek contempt as he knelt in prayer on the lowest step of the Sanctuary. Utterly lost to all but God, he embodied in visible form the prayer of the Publican. Despite the rugged asceticism of his appearance, there was a singular attraction in his simple genial manner in the parlour. He was generous and lavish in his praise of his fellow-Jesuits, and indeed of anyone of whom he believed to merit commendation.'

In 1920 and 1921 he gave spiritual exercises at the Convent of the Poor Clares, Ballyjamesduff. A member of the community gave the following impressions:

'His spirit of prayer and mortification preached even more eloquently than his words. He prayed all the time. After the last lecture, he remained on praying until the convent door was closed at 8.00 p.m. He then went straight to the town church and remained there for a long time in prayer. His spirit of mortification was wonderful. He ate very little, no meat, a little rice pudding without eggs for dinner. How he lived was a mystery. The sister who looked after his simple wants always found him absorbed in prayer when she entered the parlour. He never used the armchair, but always knelt upright on the floor.'

A retreat given by Father Sullivan in 1919 at the Sacred Heart Convent, Mount Anville, near Dublin, stands out in the memories of those who made it for the impression he left as a confessor. One of the exercitants wrote thus:

'Confessions during this retreat have remained legendary. Father Sullivan's kindness and devotedness were inexhaustible. He spent every moment between the instructions in the confessional. One soul, young and inexperienced and at that time in a state of interior distress, went to him six times, and even after the sixth effort was invited with extreme kindness and sympathy to return. However, she left the holy man this time filled with peace and consolation.'

Another added, 'It was like a mission. Everyone went to confession three or four times.'

A third said: 'I remember well the rush up to confession. All kinds of dodges were tried to get up quickly after the instructions. Some started almost before the last word had been said, others slipped out by a side door, others even hurried up the sacristy stairs to reach the chapel quicker'.

A retreat which Father Sullivan gave at the Presentation Convent, Mitchelstown, Co. Cork, in August, 1925, was marked by a series of edifying incidents some of which were not without a touch of humour.

It had been arranged that Father Sullivan should stop at the house of the parish priest, the late Archdeacon Rice, himself a most saintly man. When he presented himself at the presbytery door, his much-worn waterproof, green with age, and his equally venerable hat aroused suspicions in the mind of the housekeeper, who took him for some irregular cleric in difficulties. She summoned the Archdeacon, who full of compassion hurried down and said to Father Sullivan: 'My poor man, what can I do for you?' Father John was obliged to reveal himself, to the confusion of his kindly host, who lavished every mark of reverence on him for the remainder of his stay.

The Archdeacon was a very early riser and one morning he noticed the door of his guest's room open at an hour considerably before that of the convent Mass. Wondering where Father Sullivan had gone, he entered and found his guest asleep on the floor, with the bed untouched.

Father John's typical dry humour appeared in the manner in which he used to announce before every lecture of this retreat that some other community, contemplatives generally, were praying for the conversion of the good Sisters of Mitchelstown. 'They are praying for us in the convent of Perpetual Adoration at X,' he would announce, "so I think we'll pull through."

One morning a sister, whose cell was situated over the parlour, overheard voices conversing in loud tones. Father John had seen a poor beggarman returning from the kitchen hall, and addressed him through the window:

'Well, my poor man, have you had breakfast? Is it long since you got a chance to make your confession? Kneel down there and I'll hear you.'

And there and then, through the parlour window, Father John dispensed the riches of God's mercy and sent the poor man on his way at peace with his Maker.

One of the few retreats which Father Sullivan gave to priests was given in 1925 at the Cistercian Abbey, Roscrea. It is not surprising that Father Sullivan's austere type of retreat-giving made a strong appeal to men following a life so essentially austere. These were the recollections of one of the monks, Father Oliver:

'I can honestly say that the aggregate impression of the retreat given by Father Sullivan was just this, that one felt virtue going out from the Father Director, although every possible natural reason therefore, was utterly and palpably lacking. Father Sullivan's appearance was abject. His shrunken figure, his tense and rugged features, his time-worn and time-coloured garments, which fitted his person much as do those of a scarecrow, breathed forth an unction which was in inverse ratio to those naturally unattractive features. To this day his voice still echoes in my ears. It was raucous and absolutely devoid of intonation, but his very words come back to me precisely because they were so unadorned, so poor in phrase.

'Never yet had I seen exemplified so completely in a creature those strange boasts of St. Paul that human wisdom is folly before God, that the divine truth is not a matter of persuasive words, that the cross, the standard of Christ, is the only motive power in the world of grace.'

Father Sullivan's power of teaching by example was also very manifest during the five years which he spent (1919-1924) as Rector of the Juniorate and Retreat House at Rathfarnham Castle, on the outskirts of Dublin.

As a Superior he had certain definite shortcomings. His diffidence was such that he depended too little on his own judgment. At times he seemed not fully to realize the difficulty of the lives of his young subjects and to expect too uniform a standard of virtue. Nevertheless, the impression left on the minds of those who were in his charge at that time was a very inspiring one. His kindness was literally boundless and he was a model of every possible religious virtue.

The intensity of his life of prayer was obvious to the Juniors (as the young students are called). If any of them wished to find the Rector they always went first to the chapel. In the morning he was there before most of them. He used to say nearly all his Office in the chapel, kneeling near an open window, even in cold weather, and not resting his arms on the bench. One of the Juniors, whose room was underneath the Rector's, used to hear him praying aloud at all hours of the night. When travelling in a tram he would take off his hat and tell his beads into it with a complete lack of human respect which was rather embarrassing to the less heroic young religious who happened to be travelling with him.

The deep spirituality of their Rector was rendered all the more attractive to the young students by his unfailing kindness. One of them recalled a painful illness during which Father Sullivan did everything for him, bringing him a cup of tea every morning at 5.00 o'clock, later bringing breakfast, making his bed and attending him frequently during the day. Another whose sister was a Sister of Charity working in the Children's Hospital at Temple Street, occasionally used to ask Father Sullivan for flowers from the garden for the hospital. He was invariably told to take the best. Yet another had a brother who had been badly wounded in the First World War of 1914-18 and who was confined to bed for eleven years. Father Sullivan relaxed the usual rule against visiting friends, to the extent of allowing this young man to drop in and see his invalid brother any time he liked. He himself often called in to see the invalid and was his most anxiously expected visitor.

The same young man one day went into the Rector's room and saw to his astonishment on the bed a bottle of whiskey and a bottle of wine. 'It's all right,' said Father John. 'I'm not going on the booze. Those are for a poor old woman. They do more to keep her heart up than I can'.

During these years Father Sullivan took the deepest interest in the working-men's retreats, which had just been started at Rathfarnham. He often donned an apron and served the men at dinner. His efforts hardly helped from the practical point of view, but his charity and humility made up for his lack of skill.

8. How to Die Well

On his return to Clongowes in 1924, Father Sullivan continued for another nine years his apostolate in the countryside around, many incidents of which have already been described.

In spite of the severity of his life he always enjoyed robust health, but in later years he showed some signs of failing. Nevertheless, he was working as usual up to the beginning of February, 1933. The first sign of trouble was a swelling in his arm which had to be lanced. After this, he had to remain in the College infirmary for about a fortnight. The Matron recalled two small but significant facts connected with that time, the first that she never recalled going into his room but he was meditating on his crucifix, the second that he never rang the bell for attention except on the last morning when, as it proved afterwards, he was in danger of death.

On the morning of Friday, February 17th, he was attacked by a violent internal pain. The doctor diagnosed a dangerous obstruction and had him removed to St. Vincent's Nursing Home, Dublin. Though suffering intense agony, he received Extreme Unction with great calm before leaving, made arrangements for the saying of Masses which he had undertaken and even endeavoured to say his breviary.

He was operated on that afternoon and it was at once clear that his condition was desperate. During the remaining two days of his life, he continued to display the same extraordinary courage, selflessness and humility that had always characterized him. The surgeon who operated wrote afterwards of his 'supreme courage and fortitude.'

He spent almost the whole of the following Saturday and Sunday in prayer. Frequently one or other of the nuns in charge would say, 'Don't mind praying any more,' fearing that he would wear out the little strength left to him. His invariable reply was, 'But you pray'. Nuns and nurses alike recalled that his spirit of prayer was equalled by his marvellous patience, obedience to the slightest direction, and gratitude for the least service.

On Sunday morning, February 19th, he was able to receive Viaticum, but grew steadily weaker during the day. Some time during the afternoon, Father Roche, his Rector, who had been with him constantly during the two days, asked him to give a message to the boys at Clongowes. He whispered, 'God bless and protect them'.

His brother, Sir William Sullivan, had come over from England and was at his bedside constantly. At six o'clock he became quite unconscious. Father Roche, Sir William and Sister Thecla, the Sister of Charity in charge of the nursing home, remained with him to the end. As the night drew on Sir William began to look utterly worn out. Sister Thecla suggested that he had now done all that was possible and should go down to his club for the night. He agreed that he would wait until 11.00 p.m. and if there were no change then that he would go. It would almost seem that, at the last moment, God gave Father Sullivan one more opportunity of exercising that selflessness that had always characterized him, and of sparing his brother any further burden of weariness. At about five minutes to eleven there were signs of a change. Father Roche gave him a final absolution and he was dead at eleven o'clock, passing away most peacefully.

The next day there was a continual stream of clergy and laity touching the body with rosaries and other pious objects. The nuns of a Carmelite Convent telephoned to ask for a piece of a bandage stained with blood from the operation.

Some of the hospital students were found cutting pieces off his hair.

He was buried at Clongowes on the following Wednesday. At 9.00 a.m. Mass was celebrated by Father Roche in the People's Church. After Mass the entire congregation quite spontaneously filed up to the coffin and all, many kneeling, kissed it repeatedly, placing on it rosaries, crucifixes and prayer books. At 11.00 a.m. there was Office and Requiem Mass in the Boys' Chapel. His Lordship, Dr. Cullen, the late Bishop of Kildare and Leighlin, presided, and afterwards said the prayers at the grave. When the grave was filled in, and Bishop, priests and boys had gone, many of the people came to carry to their homes some of the clay that covered the mortal remains of him who had been such a true friend.

From this brief sketch much has necessarily been omitted. No mention has been made of Father Sullivan's teachings, or of the favours attributed to his intercession after death. For these, and for many other incidents and traits of character, the reader is referred to *Father John Sullivan, S.J.*, by the present writer (Longmans Green & Co. Ltd). By courtesy of the publishers this abridged life appears. A second biography of Father Sullivan has been published, *The Port of Tears* (Clonmore and Reynolds, Dublin) by Father Matthias Bodkin, S.J., and a documentary film, *Of Whom the World Knows Least*, has been produced by a Dublin film group.

Father John Sullivan, S.J.

In 1947 the first stage of the Process of Beatification and Canonisation, known as the Judicial Informative Process, was instituted in the archdiocese of Dublin and the diocese of Kildare and Leighlin. Father Charles O'Conor, S.J., was appointed Vice-Postulator for the Cause. In 1960 the findings of this Process were forwarded to the Sacred Congregation of Rites in Rome and are now under consideration. In autumn of the same year the remains of the Servant of God were exhumed at Clongowes Wood College in the presence of representatives of the religious and civil authorities, and transferred to a shrine in St. Francis Xavier's Church, Dublin.